She Overcame Suicide

Inspiring Stories of Serving in Ministry While Struggling with Suicide

Denise A. Kelley

Tymm Publishing LLC
Columbia, SC

She Overcame Suicide
Inspiring Stories of Serving in Ministry While
Struggling with Suicide

Paperback ISBN: 978-0-578-22170-0
Library of Congress Control Number: 2019909643

Tymm Publishing LLC
701 Gervais St, Suite 150-185
Columbia, SC 29201

Editor: Felicia Murrell
Cover Design: Tywebbin Creations

I shall NOT die, but live, and
declare the works of the Lord.
Psalm 118:17 (KJV)

Prayer

Dear Heavenly Father,

Thank you for your infinite mercies and divine grace. I ask that you will forever be with those who have been weakened by life's troubles, heaviness, and afflictions. Father, for those who were once at an end with their time here on this earth and attempted to shorten their stay by attempting suicide, I thank you for stepping in and intercepting. Your grace, mercy, and kindness are unmatchable.

Father, I'm praying for the strength of those who are suicide survivors and for those in recovery. Guide them in this hour. Lord, I pray for unity in order to provide for those who suffer in mind, body, and spirit.

Please forgive us when we, knowingly and unknowingly, ridicule, neglect, or discriminate against those who struggle with suicidal thoughts.

Father, protect and deliver those living with this sickness of the mind, whether it be emotionally, physically, or spiritually.

Guide those who research for the prevention and treatment for mental illness that leads to suicide. Hold them up with your divine compassion. Continue to keep them strong and safe in your care.

I ask you for these and other blessings in Jesus' most holy and righteous name.

Your daughter, servant and Overcomer!
Amen

Apostle Valecia D. Tigner, DD

x

Dedication

Ethel L. Kelley
Nov. 8, 1919 – Feb. 2, 1999 (Grandma)
*

George Sorkine
May 28, 1931 – Dec. 23, 2017 (Dad)
*

Melvin E. Clark
May 13, 1970 – January 9, 2018 (My Guy)

Acknowledgements

I would like to acknowledge some very special and meaningful people in my life. First of all, I always acknowledge GOD in everything I do, for truly without him I can do NOTHING! The next most important person in my life is my mother, Dora L. Sorkine. Thank you for simply doing what mothers do – JUST BEING THERE! Growing up, she taught my sisters and I that we could achieve anything if we work hard. You would think you couldn't love a person any more than you already love them, but the older I get, I find myself loving my mother more and more. My love of reading and writing stems from her.

I have a funny story, that wasn't so funny at the time. As a child whenever I was put on punishment, my mother would tell me to read a book. Let's just say I was reading a lot of books in my younger days. Although, it was from those instances that the love of reading and writing were born.

I thank my sisters, Jacqueline Kelley, Georgette Sorkine, and Gloria Jordan for being my BIGGEST supporters.

First Lady Pamela Denise Jackson for being such an inspirational, spiritual example of what a woman of God should be and of course for ALWAYS being soooo classy.

Special thanks to Ms. Ayoka Boyce for agreeing to write the foreword for this anthology. I wouldn't have had it any other way. I extend a warm thanks to all the fabulous, strong ladies that co-authored this book with me.

Last, but definitely not least, I give honor and extreme thanks to my pastor, Bishop Milton L. Hardy Sr. and First Lady Cheryl M. Hardy. These two are much more than pastor and first lady, they have become my second set of parents.

I thank my entire church family, every family member and friend for your love and support as I pursue the dream that GOD has placed inside of me. I could go on and on naming all the special people in my life that have encouraged me. If I didn't mention your name, please charge it to my head and not my heart.

Peace & Blessings
Much love to you all!

Denise A. Kelley

Table of Contents

Foreword
She Overcame Suicide

In three words, Minister Denise A. Kelley handed us the key to free many of us from the stigma and pain of attempting suicide.

I am a survivor of multiple attempts of suicide. My body has ingested horrendous amounts of pills and alcohol. Whenever those did not work, I simply reverted to my back-up plan of unhealthy living.

My body survived, but my heart and mind needed to overcome the belief that God did not love me. I don't know why I believed that I was not loved, but that thought has been with me for as long as I can remember.

I used to be angry with God. Every morning that He allowed me to open my eyes, I felt betrayed by Him.

Healing can happen immediately or over the course of time. It is okay to be in process.

If you find yourself in process, remember this, **you are an overcomer**. You have survived the thoughts and the attempts. You survived death when others succumbed. God did not betray us by giving us life, He is simply keeping His promise to give us life more abundantly.

Keep surviving.
With love and abundant life,

Min. Ayoka Boyce

CHAPTER 1

She Overcame Suicide
(Backstory)

Denise A. Kelley

SOS was my cry for help, and overcoming suicide was the outcome. *She Overcame Suicide* is not just a cute, catchy name for an acronym. *She Overcame Suicide* is the story of my life.

In my early twenties, I found myself living in a new state, new environment, and new surroundings. Moving from New York to Virginia was culture shock, but I was ready for the *newness*. I'd quickly settled in a church, which my family was already attending. I was meeting new people and establishing friendships. I was active in my new church home, and life was going good, until one day it wasn't. By the time I paid close enough attention to realize satan had strategically planted seeds of negativity, it was too late. The fruit of satan's labor had already sprung up. The lies had already been told and the rumors already in circulation. I was no longer the cool, popular young lady from New York City, I'd morphed into an outcast, and I'd become a shell of myself. The Denise I once knew was long gone.

I was never diagnosed by a medical professional, but it didn't take a PhD for me to know I was definitely depressed. Sunday after Sunday. Service after service. I would put on my *mask* and pretend like I didn't have a care in the world. At the time, I couldn't tell you why I continued to attend church, but I remained faithful to my duties and responsibilities in the ministry. Although I had no real support, I continued to teach Sunday school, usher, plan youth activities, and anything else that was requested of me. It was nothing but GOD's grace giving me the strength I needed to make it from one day to the next, literally.

As time passed, things got worse before they got better. From threatening letters on my car windshield, a busted car window, to being ridiculed. I was raised to be a strong individual, but I didn't have anyone to help me navigate this test. I could have confided in my mother or my oldest sister, but I didn't want the place where I worshiped to be viewed as anything other than righteous. A few times, I'd discussed with my pastor about the disconnection between a few of the members and myself, but I didn't want to make a big deal of it. So even in conversation with him, I didn't make it sound as serious as it really was. For that reason, I suffered alone and in silence. The *alone-ness*, and everything else associated with it, eventually became too much for me to handle by myself. It wasn't long before it took its toll on me. The breaking point presented itself one Sunday afternoon. The church went out to eat before it was time for our second service to begin. I remember sitting at the table in the restaurant with at least twenty other church members. I was attempting to hide from my pastor that the situation was much deeper than what I'd discussed with him in the past. I did this by trying my best to blend in, but it wasn't working. In sitting at that table with twenty other people, I was still ostracized. I left the restaurant and sat in my car and cried. A year had already passed since the breakdown of my relationships started. Rumors were spread that I'd said and done things people didn't like or were offended by, but I still wasn't one hundred percent sure that was the reason. I sat there trying to retrace my steps and pinpoint *when* everything went wrong. I came up with nothing, but the pain was still there. The thought entered my mind... There was only one thing left for me to do. I rummaged through my purse - found the bottle - unscrewed the cap - poured a handful of Phenergan in the palm of my hand - swallowed them all - and drove off.

　　To be continued...

CHAPTER 2

Overcame Suicide
(POEM - My Story)

Denise A. Kelley

From New York to Virginia, couldn't wait to see
what was in store.
I was starting a new chapter...walking through
a new door.

Found myself in a new home, in a new town,
In a new place of peace I'd found.

Twenty-one years old - on top of the world,
with GOD I had it all.
Twenty-one years old - on top of the world
with GOD I couldn't fall.

But then things started to turn,
Things started to get bad,
Where were those friends I thought I had?

I recalled my mother's words from when I was
a child,
"You have no friends!"
Those words were reflecting truth,
As my friendships started to end.

Months later — no longer the new kid on the
block,
True colors started seeping through, and the
smiles stopped.

I remember being in a room full of people,
and feeling like the only one there.
Remember being the outcast and nobody
cared.

Something happened,
Something went wrong.
I thought constantly, "How can this be?"
Why did those I deem family,
Turn into my enemy?

Who can right this wrong?
How can I get my church to love me again?
What can I do to fix this problem?
When did this problem even begin?

I didn't see it coming, there were no signs.
I didn't get a warning, it just snuck up from
behind.

It came out of the blue, suckered punched and
knocked to the ground.

I scrambled blindly to find safety, but safety
couldn't be found.

I tried to run from it, I tried to hide,
But what was I running from?
I tried to decide,
Then it revealed itself,
The thing that hit me was
SUICIDE

Life was happening fast, I couldn't keep up,
I tried to roll with the punches, but this thing
had me stuck.

Pain was now my new place of peace.
Suicide attempts were my new normalcy.
One attempt – two attempts –
Then a third
Fourth,
And fifth
So many attempts – I lost count
So many attempts – I couldn't keep up with

I inflicted more and more pain, in a desperate
search for relief,
but the pain kept growing and transformed into
grief.
I grieved my very existence,
I grieved every breath I took
I felt like Job,
"Lord, just erase me out of this book"
This thing had overtaken my life,
This thing had me hooked.

Singing in the choir – ushering at the door,
I put on my Sunday mask,
No one knew I was secretly praying each day
would be my last.

Yes, Saved and Sanctified,
Yet I still wanted to die.

I remember the day when it became too much,
I remember the day when I'd had enough.
It was another Sunday morning service,
I was ignored once again.
I raced to my car,
And vowed this was the end.
I will succumb to the thing,
I will let the thing win.

The prescription was written to me,
So how much harm could it be?
I took a handful of pills,
And waited — for today was the day my
existence would cease.

Repeatedly, I told myself, "Denise, just do it,
it's the only way to go,"
But with every attempt and overdose,
the answer was still NO.

"Jesus, I love you, but I can't take the pain."
I screamed and I cried.
He answered,
"Just endure a little while longer my child, I've
never left your side,

But I've predestined you to be the one to
overcome suicide."

D. A. Kelley

"I can't tell you when the thought entered my
mind of no longer wanting to remain in the
earth. Looking back, I can say it was something
that was building through the years. By the time
I realized it was a serious problem, I was in too
deep."...BUT GOD!

About the Author

D. A. Kelley is a freelance writer whose love for writing and reading began at a young age. She writes Urban Christian Fiction, which she brings to life through poetry, novels and plays. Denise's Christian plays have been performed in various locations throughout her local community.

Denise has a short story featured in *The Motherhood Diaries 2*, by national bestselling author, Mrs. ReShonda Tate Billingsley.

Denise's debut novel entitled, *70x7: The Road to Forgiveness* was originally released in 2014; but has since been re-launched with Anointed Inspirations Publishing in 2016. The new title is *Even When It Hurts: Seventy Times Seven*. This novel received a five star review. On release date, the novel was number one on Amazon's Kindle list as a Hot New Release for Urban Christian Fiction. Denise was also number two on Amazon's Kindle list for Best Seller. Denise's novella, *Revenge: Sweet as Cain*, released in December 2015, also received a five-star review from PEN 'Ashe magazine.

Denise is also a contributing author in several anthologies:

RELEASE, compiled by Saba Tekle, published July 2016.

I Still Have My Praise, compiled by Latanya Blake Allen, published July 2016.

Pain to Purpose, compiled by Tamara Marie Harris, published 2017.

Black Love Magic, Anointed Inspirations Publishing, published February 2018.

When Women Connect, compiled by Tyora Moody, released September 2018

Denise carries the message of *forgiveness* and has appeared on numerous internet radio talk shows discussing how *forgiving* changed her life, as well as other inspirational topics. Denise's ministry is geared toward encouraging hurting women.

Contact her at daknovelist@gmail.com or via her Facebook fan page, Author D. A. Kelley.

CHAPTER 3

I Just Want To Go Home

Lenai Clegg

The man that I loved for more than twenty years got married yesterday. After years of telling everyone that he would never get married with me standing right by his side, my feelings didn't matter. I don't think this had anything to do with me wanting to take my life; it wasn't one of the things on my mind at the time. But looking back, after everything happened, I realized the timing and thought it ironic. I had also just been deeply hurt by a person that I sacrificed greatly for, someone I had helped for the past year or so.

I had the strangest feeling, it was almost serene. I was not sad, mad, or even feeling the hurt and hopelessness that took refuge in every part of my being. I felt nothing. I was numb, but full of peace. It seemed strange to think that a person could have peace while planning their suicide, but that's how I felt. I was finally about to go home, to my heavenly home, where I would never be used, abused, misled, mistreated, hated on, betrayed, lied to, lied on, be talked about, abandoned, or – to sum it all up in one word, HURT, ever again.

I am a born again, Holy Ghost filled believer who was called into the ministry about fourteen years ago. I preached with power that transformed lives of those that received it. I administered the receiving of the Holy Ghost with the evidence of speaking in tongues to believers. I have sung in every choir and served as a praise and worship leader. I taught the "New Believers" class. I went door to door evangelizing, spent three and a half years of intense study to become an ordained minister and have always been a very active member in church. I have also experienced some of the worst hurt a person could feel from the leadership in the church, including mental abuse, false accusations, sexual assault, and ostracization. That was just the tip of the cold iceberg that almost caused me to drown, yet somehow, I managed to make it through all of that. But this particular day, I was tired of fighting, I was tired of being, I just wanted to go home.

I woke up, like most mornings, with a list of things that I wanted to accomplish. It was June 15, 2015, a hot summer day. I got up early and cut the hedges and cleaned the yard, then I cleaned the house, erased my phone of any incriminating pictures or messages, took a shower and put on a summer dress. I went through the day as if I was on autopilot. No music, no TV, no tears, just silence, void of any emotions, good or bad. The world of psychology would call this state of consciousness "flat".

This was not my first attempt at suicide. My first attempt happened at age fourteen, sometime after the first time I was raped and had my most prized possession, my virginity, stolen from me at thirteen-years-old. Since I was a teenager, I've contemplated suicide too many times to count, and I'm now forty-five. I've lived in a state of imagining the best ways to kill myself. Death and depression were my greatest hope and my best friend. Though no one knew. On the outside, it always looked like I had it all. I was an award winning, record setting athlete, a good student, popular, somewhat cute with a great shape, fun-loving, ambitious, fearless, creative and most of all a dedicated, proud believer. But something had been gnawing at my mind since I was a child. My parents knew that I was very sensitive and extremely critical of myself, a true perfectionist. During my difficult times, my mom would always let me know that I had a "chemical imbalance". Mental illness is not a widely accepted notion used to explain the depths of depression and extremes of energy and optimism amongst Black Christians.

It wasn't until I was thirty-eight years old that I accepted my diagnosis of Bipolar 1, Major Depressive Disorder, Anxiety Disorder and later PTSD. When I finally accepted that I had a debilitating illness that affected every aspect of my life in every way and the lives of my loved ones, I made the choice to receive help. The diagnosis came after crashing from a manic episode that lasted about six to eight months. I refused to be hospitalized, but I did agree to start taking medication and receiving therapy. My family was extremely supportive, which shocked me because I didn't think they thought I needed help. A few of my close friends, however, questioned my diagnosis and need for treatment. This was disheartening because I felt like they thought I was lying or being dramatic. The truth was, even though they had known me for most of my life and witnessed my episodes of depression, they had never been exposed to the whole picture on a consistent basis, but my family had. My extremes were just written off as me being "wild and crazy". In many ways, my friends looked up to me. So how could I have a mental illness? I was too strong for that. It's amazing how many times people have told me they thought I was "stronger than that", as if having a mental illness is a weakness. That angers me.

By the time I finished everything on my "To Do List", I turned off all the lights in the house and sat on my bed. I needed to say goodbye to the people I loved and release the culprits who contributed to my pain from any potential guilt or accountability. I wasn't mad. I wasn't seeking attention. I wanted the pain to end, and I did not want to hurt anybody in the process. This was a decision I was ready to make, and I was at peace with it.

I opened Facebook, trying to say my final goodbyes without alerting anyone that this was a suicide letter. I wanted this final act to be successful, I didn't want to be saved, I wanted to go. While writing the post, I began to cry. I could feel the pain that those who were close to me would feel. I really didn't want to hurt them, but there was no other option. I knew they would hurt for a time, but I also knew life would go on and they would heal. I've endured or participated in thirty-two years of tragic events that all led to this unbearable pain, and I still don't believe that I matter.

I posted on my Facebook page:

I just want the world to know that my mom (Mother's name) is the best mother and friend a person could ever have. She has always given unselfishly, forgiven, walked in love, never met a stranger and has always believed in me, supported me, encouraged me and loved me harder than anyone ever has. And she don't take no mess from nobody! Lol. She's a fighter surviving breast cancer and things others don't know. I thank you, Mom, for teaching me and leading me to Christ, the best gift anyone could ever give. SO strong, the things that would break other people, she gives to God and keeps it moving. She loves my dad like a queen does a king and loves my brother and son unconditionally.

Even though my dad doesn't do Facebook, I did post last Father's Day what he means to me. The man I've always looked for that would love me like he does and how he loves my mom. Dad,

21

you've been my strength, taught me how to fight, think and win and even how to forgive. I'll always be your baby girl. And my son (Son's name), the reason I felt I had a reason to live most of my life. U took care of me when I couldn't. You have such a sweet spirit and your heart is genuine. I'm so proud of the man you've become. And my brother (Brother's name), I understand ur struggles more than u know. I have always loved you and don't blame you for anything. Underneath it all, you have so much charisma, a giving heart, great personality and u are definitely a fighter. Some battles are just harder for us to fight. I get it and I love you regardless. My BFF's in this life and the next, I thank God for blessing me with true friendship. I have truly experienced God's love on earth through you guys. I'm also thankful to all of my close friends that love me and know that the love is mutual. U all have been there when my family and besties were too far away. Sometimes we get so busy and never take the time to let the people that mean the most to us know. So, I'm just letting you know. Thank u for loving me just as I am.

After completing the post, I turned off my phone and prepared for the final steps in my plan. I turned off the air conditioner so my body would decay faster, I didn't plan on anybody finding me for days. I laid out my pills, eighty-nine to be exact. I went to the kitchen and grabbed the almost empty bottle of wine from the top of the fridge. I don't drink, but my parents left it on their last visit, and I knew it would probably shock my system, especially when mixed with the pills. I was hoping this would be a deadly combination. Taking the pills was harder than I thought it would be. There were so many and I didn't have enough wine to swallow them all, so I went to get a warm glass of water. Finally, I forced down all the medication I had saved from the past couple of months.

On top of my pretty comforter, in my hot bedroom, I began to talk to God. "Daddy, if this doesn't work, then I will know without a doubt that you still have a purpose for me." My eyes closed from heaviness, and my body felt weightless. I kept thinking that I was going to see this "light", but I didn't. Instead, I saw myself lying on my bed. *Why is it so cold in here? I'm freezing.* I wanted to get under the covers but I couldn't move. I heard my breathing get slower and slower and slower until I no longer heard it. There was complete silence. I was not afraid, but I wondered what was happening. *Why am I still here? Oh no, I have to pee badly.* I couldn't move, and I was really cold. *Oh, if I could just get to the bathroom.* I wasn't sure how long I had been laying on top of my comforter. At some point, I heard the young lady who lived downstairs knocking on my front door. I had taken her into my home to help get her life together.

"Ms. Lenai, Ms. Lenai, are you here? Where are you? Oh God, please don't let anything be wrong." I heard her say.

I watched her go past my room looking for me, then she doubled back and found me on the floor, laying in a puddle of urine.

"Oh no, Ms. Lenai, please don't be dead, please don't be dead. Wake up, Ms. Lenai!"

She struggled to lift my lifeless body up off the floor, and we both fell on the bed. She called 911 and a mutual acquaintance. The paramedics rushed in and tried to revive me. I heard one guy say, "She barely has a pulse, but she's alive."

Something cold went under my nose and another medic was holding my head, telling me to open my eyes.

"You can do it. I know you can, open your eyes for me," he coached.

I don't know how I did it, but I cracked one eye open enough for him to see it.

They asked the girl what happened, and she told them she lived downstairs and she hadn't heard any movement upstairs all night. When morning came, she decided to check on me before she went to work because I wouldn't answer the phone. Apparently, what seemed like thirty minutes was really more like twelve hours. The young girl said she used her key to get in and found me on the floor, and that I must have taken the pills from these empty bottles.

I was rushed to the hospital by ambulance and remained in the intensive care unit for several days until I was able to walk again. The nurses had to do everything for me. They had to roll my big behind over to put the bedpan underneath me to pee and wipe me, all while a stranger assigned to watch me 24/7 sat in a chair beside me. I guess because I had tried to commit suicide.

The only family I had in Roanoke was my son and my brother. My brother also suffers from mental illness and was not currently communicating with me or my son. So, my baby was really the only one I had here. When I was able to communicate, I told the young lady not to call the pastor. I did not trust the church anymore (because of several things that had recently taken place). My parents and my son were notified. My parents took the first plane out of Florida, and my son arrived at my bedside. With tears of pain in his eyes, he said, "I love you, Mama. I don't want you to die. I need you, so many people love you." It hurt my heart to see him crying with such fervor and agony. I never want to see that pain in his eyes again.

After a few days, I was moved to the mental hospital on the fourth floor, which was the highest level of care and reserved for the sickest patients. I had been there several times before, so I knew the protocol. I talked to my mom on the phone every day, while her and my dad stayed at my house. Finally, I was able to receive visitors, and I was so happy to see my parents when they came. I wanted to go home so bad, but my evil doctor was so mean and refused to release me. He said I was not ready and that I had to earn the trust back. After several days, I had another breakdown when he refused to let me go home to be with my family. I knew my parents couldn't stay long because they had to get back to work, and I wanted to be with them and my son.

After a few more days, I was promoted to the third floor, which was one step closer to home. There, I had more freedom and could wear my own clothes. I was still sick and having nightmares. Every time I lay my head down to rest, in my mind, I could feel my body dying as if the suicide attempt was still taking place. I stayed in my room the first couple of days because I didn't want to be around anybody, including the evil doctor who was holding me captive against my will, but I knew the only way I would be released was to participate in the therapy classes throughout the day. Each day, my parents and my son visited, and my parents noticed when I was not doing well and when I started to improve. I felt the same throughout the entire stay.

After almost two weeks, I was released to go home and I was elated. But everything at home seemed different. There was no doubt that my life had been forever changed by this experience. As I sat with my mom, going over my finances, we discovered I had let everything go and was behind on everything, something I never did. I was very diligent about paying my bills and constantly increasing my credit score. It had been months since I paid things, and I didn't even know it. I had been experiencing mania and depression throughout the last year, so everything was off kilter. I was so embarrassed. My mom sat with me as I struggled to remember passcodes, processes and bills due. My mind was not operating the way it used to. As a college graduate with a B.A and an M.B.A in Business Administration, a successful business owner of over fourteen years developing self-esteem workshops in Roanoke City Schools, a talented beautician/barber/instructor, I couldn't even take care of myself. I was so afraid to drive, the anxiety was unbearable. Everything frightened me, even being around people.

After a few days, my parents had to leave, and then the struggle really began. I barricaded myself in my house and only allowed my son and his girlfriend in. My house was a mess. I couldn't clean, bathe, cook or do anything but sleep, cry and eat junk. I talked to my best friends, who were there the whole way, being supportive, calling me at the mental hospital, and praying without ceasing, even through their pain. I found out tons of people knew about my suicide attempt, it was the talk of the salons and barbershops. I continue to be hurt by people who found my illness and desperation a major source of entertainment. I was a public figure of sorts. I worked on a radio show, was known for health and fitness throughout the community and known for being a standout beautician/barber and teacher. I was very outgoing and fun; the type of individual "haters" couldn't wait to see fall.

Three and a half years later, I am still recovering. The first six months after coming home from the hospital were the hardest of my life. Going outside on the back porch for five minutes a day was sometimes impossible. Nobody knows the pain and the struggle of living after attempting to take your own life. Through a rock-solid support system, prayer, therapy and medication, I have been able to move forward and heal. I cannot say that I will never attempt suicide again, because with this illness, sometimes a person's thoughts take over logic and will. But I know my triggers, and I have a support system to turn to when I feel myself getting out of control.

I have decided to tell my story as a testimony of what God can and will do, even against our own will. He is the way, the truth and the life (John 14:6), and He will never leave nor forsake you – NEVER. I know my purpose is yet to be completely fulfilled because God told me that by not letting me die. I still have not decided to go back to church, but I am constantly seeking to know God better for myself. I believe that my ministry is outside of the church, without a title or fame. I no longer seek to be recognized, be great or be out front. I want to help hurting people who are without hope. I want to be a witness to people of God's love, grace and mercy, unearned through actions or anything we say. I am learning every day that my success is not defined by the world's standards (not even family or friends), but by my relationship with my Father who abides within me. During the toughest time of my life, God showed me what was truly important — not owning things, popularity, money, great achievements or any of that. RELATIONSHIP is the most important thing in life. Relationship with him, with family, with friends and with others. People can die and be saved because of relationship. When I had nothing to give, the people who loved me the most showed up. I will never forget the love I experienced in my darkest hour by those who truly cared for me without judgment or shaming. They gave, looking for nothing in return and will be there to do it all again, no matter what I'm going through. God uses people to demonstrate His love. He is worthy of ALL my praise. There is none like Him. I wanted to escape the loneliness and pain and go home to be with my heavenly Father so badly, forgetting that He abides in me and I in Him, and that home is wherever He is. I am thankful that He is patient with me and forgiving as I go through this daily walk. I know what love looks like, because I have sat in His presence and communed with Him. Therefore, I strive daily to BE love to those that hurt me and those that love me back. I am home.

About the Author

Lenai Clegg is a Coatesville, PA, native who currently resides in Roanoke, VA. She is the mother of one son, Kyree Clegg. Lenai attended Morgan State University and Mary Baldwin College. She holds a B.A in Business Management with an emphasis in Human Resources and a M.B.A from Averett University.

Lenai has a heart for individuals who suffer with mental illness. She is a Peer-to-Peer trainer for National Alliance on Mental Illness (NAMI). Lenai is CEO/founder of Nevaeh Services. This business is geared toward mentoring and empowering young ladies to live their best life. Lenai is also a licensed cosmetologist, but she's not just your normal hair stylist. She has a self-esteem program designed to teach children to love themselves through the concepts of cosmetology. This program was instituted in the Roanoke City Schools system and has been successfully active for fourteen years.

Lenai is a Christian and is active in ministry. She shows her devotion to her faith by evangelizing, teaching and preaching the Word of GOD.

This is Lenai's first co-authored book, but it won't be her last. Lenai plans to speak out on various platforms in order to motivate and encourage young women.

CHAPTER 4

Jes Push Pause Breathe Again

Jesta Bouie

Are you serious? Why me, God? Why this again? I don't get it, this hurts too bad. These are a few of the thoughts that ran through my brain. How do you go from being in a committed, serious relationship – engaged one day to NOTHING? A complete stop sign. How could a man turn love off like a light switch or blow it out and just walk away? I listened to you, God. I waited, I let you heal my heart. I let my walls down once again. You know what I've been through, and yet, I trusted again, loved again, opened my heart and all of me – the complete me – my entire soul, heart, spirit, being, the essence of me...again.

This cannot, CANNNNNNNOTTTTT be real. I can't go through the shame and embarrassment again, God. I am a complete fool to have not seen the signs, or did I see them and ignore them? Were there any signs, God? I just don't get it. What did I do to deserve this? This kind of heartbreak, this kind of deception. THIS LIE! Please answer me, God, please.

A very faint but small, still, smooth voice, that sounds familiar but feels not real, whispered in the area behind my ear, "He AIN'T going to answer you. He never really has, look at your life, just look at it. It's NOT been a walk down a golden path. Who has ever truly loved you, not even your own mother or father? No one has ever really claimed you. No one in your family fully claims you until they need something from you. Your own mother did not believe you as a child when you told her the man touched you and was touching you. Then she stayed and lived a happy life and replaced you with his daughter." My mind started racing, flooded with all kinds of thoughts and visual memories playing like an old picture movie at a drive-in theater of so many hurtful things from my past. A two-dimensional movie that as time goes by turns into 3D technicolor. All the abuse from my birth mother, being told that she tried to abort me before I was born. My birth father's mother telling the community and declaring in court, "That bastard ain't none of my clan!" All of the acts of molestation that occurred, my birth mother lying and saying it was a figment of my imagination — still holding on to that lie today. The fact that she chose him over me and helped raise his only child while my grandmother raised me by herself. The way my family has always said they loved me, but their actions never seemed to show love. I always felt like I was tolerated and not a real part of the family because my great-aunt, whom I grew up calling "Mama Jessie" chose to raise me after her sister, my maternal grandmother, died years before I was ever thought of. I was picked on and talked about because everyone knew about my mother's lifestyle and felt sorry for the one child she had but couldn't raise.

After God called my last king home to glory on July 13, 2014, I finally thought I had been found again by a real man of God, the king God had set aside just for me. He was such a gentleman when we first met, always making sure I was protected and provided for. He professed his love, and I figured if he could handle knowing all my history and it not affect how he felt about me, then he was a keeper.

I didn't believe in fairytales, based on the past track record of my love life, but one of my friends told me to open my mind to the idea of dating again. I had already met a couple of gentlemen from one site and had great dates. I could honestly say the good dates turned into great friendships, but I was not feeling creating another profile. Nevertheless, my friend talked me into creating a profile on a Black Christian dating website, and a few weeks later, I received a message that my picture was liked. I responded with a "thank you," and the conversation started from there.

After a few days of messaging back and forth on the site, answering questions like who are you and where are you from, I thought we might possibly be related based on his last name and the area he said his family was from. I called my mama to make sure there was no possible way we could be related on either side of my family. He asked me out on a date and let me pick the location. His response completely floored me when I told him I would meet him at my favorite restaurant. He said, "Oh no, ma'am, I am old school and very old-fashioned, and this is a real date. I am coming to your house to pick you up. If I need to ask your sons can I take you out and have you back at a very decent hour, that is okay too," and then he asked, "Can you be ready by six or do you need more time after you get off work?" While this is how the fairytale started, it ended in a complete nightmare.

Ten months later, on February 23, 2018, I received a text from my fiancé telling me he needed space because we were going in two completely different directions. I thought the text was a joke, that perhaps his cousin had finally talked him into playing a prank on me. How could he send me a message like that when we had created a life together? We went to church together, we shopped together, we planned our week, our month, our everything out together. We were engaged. We had just sat down in my living room with two budgets and combined them into one, so I was completely confused.

After buying me an iPhone so we could Facetime, he was no longer responding to my messages. I had been very content and happy with my android. All of this felt so unbelievable, like what in the world? Are you freaking kidding me? I knew if I didn't pray, I would need bail money for my actions.

He told me to keep the truck I was driving, the one he gave me, and the iPhone I was using, the one he bought me. Beyond that, minutes passed with no response. Hours, days —no response. He said he just needed space to think. But after much prayer, God started speaking and told me there was a lie in the midst. I couldn't go to church because I was joining his church and we were planning to have our wedding there before the end of the year. I tried to pray, but I had no words. My heart felt like it shattered into a million pieces. I called my mother in tears, she could not understand it either. My best friends were baffled. No one knew what was really going on.

He had ridden in on a white horse, my black Prince Charming for ten months. When I thought there couldn't possibly be another after the death of my king, he came along. He completely changed me — slowed me down, protected me, professed his undying love to me for all to hear. And then just like that, he was gone.

Depression entered like a tsunami and I didn't want to live anymore. I started hearing conversations, got wind of things being said. I heard his voice so clearly having a conversation about me lying, saying I asked him for money and other things. Things I never asked for, things I never asked him to do. I had been longing to hear from him since he sent me that first text on Friday, February 23, 2018, telling me he needed space, and the sound of his voice sent me into a downward spiral. A love that is real does not involve deception on any level. I had been lied to, but I didn't know the intention or reason behind the lie.

After crying myself to sleep for many nights or not sleeping at all, I wanted it all to end. I did not want to live and have to continue to try and figure out where I went wrong or what I did or did not do. The devil had so many suicidal thoughts running through my mind, my thought process was completely jacked up. I had no desire to get up, and I was completely drained. Once again, my heart was shattered because I put my trust and my all in a DAMN man. A man after God's own heart, or so he said, his family said, his friends said, his church family said, his co-workers said, everyone co-signed and vouched for this man being who he said he was. Ugh!

I spent another night waking up to a pillow drenched from tears and another day walking around as a barely functioning, depressed Black woman. I hardly remembered the events from the day before even though I had just preached at a women's conference. I completed the work and left empty, but it was truly on God that day. I did not want to live without being loved the way I had experienced for the past ten months. Was it all a dream? If so, it was turning into my worst nightmare because I had no answers from him. He would not call or answer my calls, only text messages. We scheduled a time to sit down and talk, and he didn't show up. I had never experienced true love my entire life from anyone, so why not end it?

I hadn't been feeling well for a few weeks, everyone knew I was sick. No one was planning to stop by, and my family wouldn't call unless they needed something. My kids weren't home, so I didn't have to worry about my daughter coming in to find me. I planned to dial 911. By the time they arrived and kicked the door in, it would be too late. I had a half full bottle of sleeping pills and a cold can of something in the refrigerator to wash them down. With a fist full of pills, I cried out to God. "Tell me why should I not go through with this if you have need of me so much? You can't have need of me when I want to end it all. Everyone who says they love me has hurt me. Why God? Why did you make me this way? What did I do to deserve this? Each and every time I open my heart, betrayal happens. How can I minister to your people feeling like this? How I can minister wanting to end my own life? Why did you allow me to live when my mother tried to abort me and I died twice that same day? Why, for a life filled with so much heartache and pain?

JUST, PUSH, PAUSE AND BREATHE AGAIN

I heard the words so softly. My phone rung and it was one of my besties from high school. A text message from another popped up at almost the exact same time. She called, and I let it go to voicemail. My phone rang again right after that call, and it was one of my spiritual big sisters leaving me an encouraging word. Then another one inboxed me on Messenger and told me to please call her because she was planning her first women's conference and not only did she want me to speak, she needed my assistance as well. But the one call that made me flush the pills down the toilet was from my only daughter. My little princess called and said, "Hey, Mommy, I love you and don't know what I would do without you in my life."

A still, small calm but deep voice said, "My child, this is why I have need of you and the reason I birthed need in you! A small package with such a powerful voice, just speak my truth while speaking yours! I loved you before I formed you!"

Repentance fell all over me, and with a very heavy heart, I fell to my knees and asked for complete forgiveness, rededicating my life back into his hands. All I could do in that moment was thank God for keeping my mind.

Two scriptures came to my mind right after I finished praying and having a moment of praise and worship. "Trust in the Lord with all your heart, And lean not on your own understanding" (Proverbs 3:5) and Jeremiah 3:33, "Call to Me, and I will answer you, and show you great and mighty things, which you do not know."

When God has need of you, he always finds a way to remind you of why he has need of you. The need of you is greater than any trial, tribulations, obstacle, situation, or circumstance. No denial, break up, heartbreak, letdown, false accusation, lie, deception, foolishness, or anything that is not of his will or way can change the call of God on your life. Each and every individual in ministry is a human first who has a real life and goes through real things just like every other individual in church. Life is life and there is not one person on Earth who does not have a life to live.

Lord, I thank you for my life - for the push, pause and being able to breathe again for your glory to be revealed in my life.

Love,

your daughter Jes – Jes Speaking Truth Boldly

About the Author

Jesta Shon Trice Bouie, also known as Jes Speaking Truth, has been a motivational speaker against domestic violence for over twenty-five years and is a sought after empowerment speaker for women and youth. While wearing many other hats in and around her local community, church and family, she also serves as a high school business education teacher, assistant coach, and mentor. A mother of three— two adult sons and a ten-year old daughter whom she loves to life, Jes is also a survivor of abuse, neglect, domestic violence and so much more. She currently resides in Greensboro, North Carolina, and does not mind telling anyone about the goodness of God in her life.

She has been involved in church ministry for over twenty-seven years and accepted her call into ministry in 2000 as an ordained deaconess but did not stop there. In 2012, she was ordained as a minister, and after many years of running from her calling, in 2018, she accepted her mantle as a prophetess under the mentorship/ leadership of Apostle Alicia Foust of Ignited Blue Apostolic Church International. Jes fully walks in the prophetic as an authentic voice - speaking only what God tells her. She wants people to be delivered, restored, reconciled and set free to be what God has called them to be. She understands the plight of the rejected, set aside, looked over and the forgotten but knows that God has a purpose for everything that happens in life. Her goal is that God's will be done while encouraging people to JUST BREATHE again when life gets hard.

CHAPTER 5

The Woman, The Wife, The God Seeker

Nicole Twitty

You are the one that possesses the keys to your being. You carry the passport to your own happiness. - Diane Von Furstenberg

I was having the worst day of my life, and I was dealing with some heavy life issues that made me question who I was as a woman, wife, and lover of God. I sought to please Him in every area of my life daily, but this day I felt empty, frustrated, sad, unhappy, and livid. I found myself at a place in life that I didn't understand, and I had lost all sense of direction and guidance about how my life had turned out. I was a God-fearing woman that prayed about everything that concerned my life, and I believed God to work it out for my good and His glory. I was taught at a young age by both grandmothers that a good woman, wife, and mother took all her issues and problems to God and left them there knowing He would work them out. **"Rejoicing in hope, patient in tribulation, and continuing steadfastly in prayer" (Romans 12:12, NKJV).**

It was how all the women that had a positive role in my life stayed above the fray and coped with their daily duties. I had watched my grandmothers handle life. They just kept going, providing for their families and from the outside, they seemed happy. I heard them hum hymns and 'talk' to themselves. I later found out they were talking and singing praises unto the Lord. **"Praise the Lord! For it is good to sing praises to our God; For it is pleasant, and praise is beautiful" (Psalm 147: 1, NKJV).** I took up that same trait and followed the same routine daily. There were days it made me feel like pressing on in life, but this day was different. Tears wouldn't stop rolling down my face. I couldn't understand it. I had gathered all the information from everything I learned from the women I trusted and gleaned from and it had worked so well for me all my life.

But this day was different, and I couldn't make the feelings I was experiencing go away. I thought I would choke on the knot in my throat. With every breath I tried to take, the pain I felt worsened. My heart felt like it was coming out of my chest, and my mind wouldn't stop thinking about how hurt and devastated I felt. Life had beat me down and left me lonely and lifeless. There was not one happy thing that I could think of to make the strange feelings stop — not one hymn to hum or one moment I could recall that had been good in my life. I had nothing left inside of me to pray about. I felt empty, numb, isolated, and emotionally disconnected to what I knew as my life. I loved my life and family, but this day nothing connected me to that life. I was overwhelmed by my sorrows, brokenness, and sadness.

What I was dealing with was too much for me to handle, and I had no one that I could talk to because I was raised that women sought the Lord, and wives never told their business to anyone outside their homes. I could hear my grandmothers in my head telling me that was frowned upon. I had learned their instructions well and behaved accordingly. I spent all my time and energy building my family instead of seeking friends. I watched my grandmothers deal with all their family affairs and never show any signs of what I was displaying. I had watched my mother deal with life and handle all her ups and downs and keep moving with her daily duties and activities as a mother. I felt like everybody would see me as a disappointment, a failure. Why would they not feel that way about me when I felt that way about myself? I had tried to be the best woman I could be. I had tried to be the best wife I could be. I had tried to seek God and do what I felt would be pleasing in His sight. I took care of my children. I did everything a wife does to take care of her home. Why was I feeling so abused and beat up by everything I did right?

I couldn't understand what was happening, and the feeling was so intense it made my headache. The non-stop pounding was so severe I thought I would pass out. I was disappointed and ashamed of myself. I felt like a fake, like I had somehow brought all of this on myself. In between crying uncontrollably and trying to breathe, I remember thinking to myself that maybe everyone would be better off without me. For the life of me, I could not think of anything else I had to give or offer. I was depleted and over it all. I looked around my home and realized I didn't connect with it emotionally any more. I thought everyone I cared for didn't need me to play that role for them anymore. I felt alone, abandoned, afraid, lifeless and unloved. Why was I feeling this way? How did my life turn out to be like this after I gave all I had to do for others?

I stood in the middle of my bedroom glancing over my home to see everything my hands took care of, and in that moment, it all made me sad. What once made me happy and secure now made me sad and lonely. I recall looking for medicine to take because all the emotions, feelings, and pain made my head hurt more. I remembered the medicine I was looking for was in my purse. I grabbed the bottle of pills, slid down on the floor at the foot of my bed and poured all that was left of them in my hand. My eyes filled with tears that blinded my vision. I reached up and wiped my eyes to glance over my home yet again, hoping maybe one more glance would give me some sense of direction. Nothing but a wave of pain stronger than before rushed over me. I laid my head back against the bed and looked up.

I JUST WANT THE PAIN TO STOP NOW!

I looked down at all the pills in my hand. Unable to stop crying, I raised my hand to my mouth and poured all the pills inside, chasing them with a sip of water. I just couldn't take it anymore, I needed what I was feeling to stop. I picked up my phone and sent a message to certain loved ones saying, I love you and I'm sorry. I just can't do this anymore. At that moment I felt myself going out, I heard my daughters calling my name, trying to get me off the floor. Frantically, they grabbed me and put me in the car as I heard them crying my name. I drifted in and out of consciousness. I remember hearing my daughter talking to a nurse on her cell phone as she drove me to the Emergency Room. They told me later the lady on the other end of the phone said please don't let her fall to sleep. Both of my girls screamed my name, and their screams broke something inside of me that emotionally I hadn't felt in a while. In that moment, I thought to myself *what did I just do?*

My baby girl climbed over the front seat and sat beside me, shaking my body to keep me from going to sleep. Her voice sounded so distant, but I kept hearing her say, "Mama... Mama... Mama." Something in her voice gave me the strength to pray, God please don't let me die.

I'm alive today to let you know that God still has need of you. Your life story of events has purpose and power to change someone's life even now. I didn't know there was more that

49

God was requiring from my life and what I was feeling was birthing pains for my next assignment in life. **For I know the thoughts that I think toward you, says the Lord, thoughts of peace and not of evil, to give you a future and hope (Jeremiah 29:11, NKJV).**

God had another plan for my life. He wasn't finished using me for His glory. I'm so grateful and thankful that He didn't allow my attempt at suicide to succeed. I had more ministry to do. I had more teaching to give. I had more women I needed to reach for His kingdom. I had more to impart into my own daughters that no one had taught me until I experienced it for myself. I realized some things I had to experience couldn't be taught by others, I had to catch it through the revelation of God. I didn't understand that what doesn't kill you in life will make you stronger. My life, my experiences, my walk with God was training me how to truly withstand hardship like a good soldier, so that I could pull other women from the grasp that hell (trials, hardship, and tribulations) had on them. **For I consider that the suffering of this present time are not worthy to be compared with the glory which shall be revealed in us (Romans 8:18, NKJV).**

Me overcoming suicide was to help you understand that giving up is not an option. I don't care what you are facing in life, you are not alone, and yes, God cares about you. The pain, hurt, disappointment, frustration, heartbreak, depression, and brokenness, God can heal. Life is hard, yes, but you can survive it through proper guidance and trustworthy help. Trust your process, even when you feel like it's taking your breath away. I know you don't understand it, and you feel like you can't take any more of it. Please, trust God in it and find trustworthy friends, mentors, life coaches and professional help that can guide you through what you are feeling. You don't have to deal with depression, anxiety, fear or hurt alone. As I began to rebuild my life after overcoming the attempt to commit suicide, I never could have known or imagined that God would use my life and what I had been through as a beacon of light to help other women challenge their thinking and come out of issues they were facing.

My life was saved to tell you who are reading this now that you can live through it. God has more planned for your life on the other side of your dilemma. Choose life today and opt out of giving up; He will give your life and life more abundantly. **"1 am come that they might have life, and that they might have it more abundantly (Romans 8:18, NKJV).**

God wants you to have superabundance of life, full of joy and strength for your mind, body, and soul. It is the enemy's job to keep you full of hurt, pain, aggravation, and resentment to frustrate you from your God given purpose. You are more than what you've been through. You are more than what has hurt you. You are more than what you tell yourself. You are more than what others have said to you or how they have treated you. You are powerful in your own right, even standing in the issues you are facing today. Tell yourself that you can do this because you trust a God that is almighty and has all power to pull you out of what you're in today. I don't care how you are feeling just know if you live through it, there is purpose in your pain. This same pain you are feeling will fuel you to pull others through. Keep pushing and fighting for your life daily. It isn't over until you've completed your assignment for God. It hurts now, but it will empower you later. Nobody said life was easy, but God promised that He would see you through it all.

Learn to put all your trust in God and seek to please Him daily. When you seek to please people and it's not reciprocated back, it hurts your feelings and you tend to regret that you did a good deed before the Lord. People may never be satisfied with what you do or appreciate you for your efforts, but if you do your good works before the Lord because it's the right thing to do, He will reward you for them. I carried around so much pain and frustration because I felt used, abused, and neglected for many years of my life.

When you put expectation of what you want in return for life, you set yourself up for failure and disappointment.

Take your power back and learn to appreciate yourself. Live happy being able to choose to do what's pleasing to the Lord.

Trust in the Lord, and do good; Dwell in the land, and feed on His faithfulness. Delight yourself also in the Lord, And He shall give you the desires of your heart.

Commit your ways to the Lord, Trust also in Him. And He shall bring forth your righteousness as the light, And your justice as the noonday. Rest in the Lord, and wait patient for Him; Do not fret because of him who prospers in his way, Because of the man who brings wicked schemes to pass. Cease from anger and forsake wrath; Do not fret-it only causes harm (Psalm 37: 3-8, NKJV).

You are the woman, the wife, and the God seeker that has power and strength to pull through your hardship. Your life has trained you to come out and be better than you've ever been.

About the Author

Elder Elect Lady Nicole Twitty is a woman after God's heart, wife, mother of three, grandmother of one, leader, teacher, and entrepreneur. Elect Lady Twitty inspires women and young girls to live out Proverbs 23:7, "For as he(she) thinks in his(her) heart, so is he(she)," and to be all they have been called to be in God by helping them understand if you change the way you think, you can change the way you live. Gifted by God to heal, Elect Lady Twitty is the ministry leader of Women of Destiny and Daughters of Destiny Ministries and the First Lady of Word of Deliverance. She, herself, has walked in a life of pain only to experience the healing hand of God that she might be a vessel of healing for many.

Leading the women of God with empowering lessons on building women and relationships, Elect Lady Twitty understands that issues don't just start when we become women, they start as daughters of destiny and if we don't learn how to grow healthy in the Lord, we become women with issues. It is her vision to produce kingdom women of destiny, and she is determined to build women of character, integrity, good relationships, friendships, unobstructed vision, entrepreneurship, and women with a heart for God's people.

She has challenged the women at Word of Deliverance Church to create BALANCE in all areas of their lives mentally, physically, and spiritually while maintaining stability and not becoming overwhelmed.

Elect Lady Nicole Twitty's vision is to continue educating, equipping, and empowering the women and daughters of God to be servants for the kingdom.

CHAPTER 6

Footsteps to My Suicide

Tresser Henderson

I never saw suicide and me going hand and hand, but life is a finicky thing like that. Growing up, I never thought I would ever think about taking my own life. But life kicks in and eventually, I became a vessel of thoughts for doing something tragic which would affect many surrounding me. And I knew they wouldn't understand because I didn't understand myself. I felt like I was a terrible person, someone who was weak and not worthy of the life God had blessed me with. How could I feel this way when I had children? The battle within overwhelmed me to the point where I thought I was crazy.

After the birth of my first child, I noticed how different my thoughts were. I was sad, moody, tired, and cried all the time, but I thought this was how you were supposed to feel after giving birth. Later, my co-worker Lisa, a nurse practitioner diagnosed me with a severe case of postpartum depression, which explained why I was not feeling a connection with my baby. Finding this out was a relief, but I stayed in denial thinking it would eventually subside and even go away. Unfortunately, I was wrong.

With each high-risk pregnancy and the birth of each child, my depression got worse. Thankfully, all my children were healthy and seemed good. At least, that's what I wanted everyone to see, but there came a point when I didn't want to get out of bed. All I wanted to do was sleep with the curtains drawn and the door closed, wishing everyone would leave me alone. My mood was all over the place. Everything and everyone around irritated me, including my husband and children. I was overburdened by my responsibilities. Even though I had a husband, I was the main one responsible for our family. As every woman knows, moms do way more than dads.

Pretending everything was okay eventually pushed me deeper into depression, and during a visit back home, I considered taking my life. My children were in good hands with their grandparents and I was on my way back from running an errand for my mother. It was dark and I remember thinking all I had to do was jerk the steering wheel to the right and plow my car into one of the many oak trees which flanked the road I was on. All I could think about was how tired I was and how tired I was of trying. I wanted to end it all. I argued with God in my mind, even chastising him for these thoughts and not having the energy to fight or struggle anymore. Being a woman was hard enough but placing wife and motherhood on top of that made things a lot more difficult for me.

As if God knew how serious I was about this act of taking my own life, my children entered my mind and tears began to stream down my face. Everything I did in my life was because of them. They were my entire world. This was not a burden I wanted to add to their lives. I didn't want them to think I didn't love them enough to live for them, so I decided to live. As easy as that sounds, this was not an easy choice for me. Every day was a struggle to put one foot in front of the other. I didn't understand how crippling my depression was. I made the decision to see my doctor who thought it was a good idea to be placed on medication. But I declined. I thought I was stronger than depression and could handle it. How wrong was I?

The stigma placed on individuals who took medication for mental health led me to decline the help I needed. The hometown I grew up in was not only small, it was also small minded. People frowned upon medication and even counseling that pertained to getting help for anything mental, unless the counseling came from someone in ministry. It took me years to get the help I needed. Coming from a family with a history of addiction, I was afraid of getting hooked on medication, but my mother told me I needed help and thought it might be a good idea to consider taking it. By then, I'd advanced to another job, and I didn't have Lisa to help me along the way. But God placed another doctor in my life, Dr. Adkins, who was just as knowledgeable and caring about my situation. Still, I declined the help for fear of being judged. Worried about me, my mother stayed on top of my condition. She knew I was stressed beyond measure and needed to get a handle on things. She was aware that I had been diagnosed with depression but had no clue that I had thoughts of taking my own life. I might have said I was fine, but my mother knew better and asked someone to intervene on my behalf.

My mother's best friend (and my husband's cousin), Minister Patricia Liggon, called me one day. She told me my mom was concerned about me and wanted her to talk to me. I was hesitant about sharing my personal life with her but eventually opened up. Though, I held on to the secret that I wanted to take my life.

Minister Liggon changed my life. "Would you take medication for high blood pressure?" She asked, and I said yes. "Would you take medication for high cholesterol or diabetes?" Again, I answered yes. Then she asked, "Then, why wouldn't you take medication for your depression?" I didn't have an answer for that, but a light bulb went off. Not only did she help me see it was okay to get the help I needed, she also confided that she too was dealing with depression and taking medication for it as well. I decided to get the help I needed, and with Dr. Adkins' assistance, I found a medication that worked for me.

Several years have passed since that crucial phone call, and I'm doing much better. God sent people into my life to direct me down the road I needed to go. One of the main reasons I was so hesitant to take medication was because of the stigma in the African American community and church. I actually had a cousin tell me I needed to pray the depression away and that the reason I couldn't shake the devil of depression was because my faith wasn't strong enough. This truly messed with my head, especially when I was raised in the church to believe this. Everything could be prayed away. And thinking this way almost cost me my life.

I do know prayer can fix things. God will forever be limitless in his grace and mercy. It's the people who warped the scripture, making us fear what may happen if we did it this way or didn't do it that way that don't seem to be limitless in their grace and mercy. Some Christians, who are more accepting and forgiving of people coming to church with afflictions like alcoholism and drug use, frown upon depression as if it is not an affliction also. They think depression is you just being sad or tired or even weak, and this angered me.

Minister Liggon, who I now called Ms. Pat, invited me to be a speaker at a woman's prayer breakfast at my home church because she felt depression was never discussed within the church. I was honored and jumped at the chance to do this as it gave me the opportunity to tell individuals about my battle with depression. Our community underestimates how depression affects individuals. I was nervous about how my presentation would be received by most of the older women who had this old school way of thinking, but this was an opportunity for me to educate them on something that was being swept under the rug for generations. And I was willing to shine a light on that at the cost of me revealing personal things about myself.

My mother and Ms. Pat were so proud of me. And even though I felt proud of what I accomplished, I could see my speech was not received well by a lot of the older women in the church, but that was fine with me. I was in a comfortable place in my life where their opinions didn't affect me anymore.

After I spoke, Ms. Pat asked if anyone wanted to respond or ask questions. A couple of people said something that fell in line with praying my depression away, but another elevation happened in my life when this young lady stood.

The young lady was in a college studying to become a nurse. She too had moved away from our small town and, like me, was visiting this particular Saturday. She was in tears when she stood and couldn't hardly speak. She testified about how stressed she was with working and going to school and how she didn't think she could do it anymore. I understood what she was going through because I had been where she was. She shared how she'd contemplated committing suicide. Of course, this got the church's attention. Eyes widened and many clutched their pearls. Mumbles rumbled throughout the space at her boldness to admit something like this. I thought she was very courageous. I rose from my seat next to my mother and smiled at the young lady with tears in my eyes and for the first time in my life, I admitted that I too had contemplated suicide.

Not only did she look surprised by my revelation, my mother was stunned. I hated for my mother to find out that way, but I knew this was the time to speak my truth. I didn't want this young lady thinking she was crazy or alone in her way of thinking. Even though I had talked about the signs of depression and even mentioned suicide in my speech, I never admitted I wanted to do this. The Lord told me to tell my truth. This moment wasn't happenstance. This was God placing the two of us in the same place at the same time for this reason. And if he gave her the courage to speak about her thoughts, then I needed to acknowledge her by admitting my own.

I testified that the only reason I was still amongst the living was because of my children. To say she and I shocked the church members was an understatement. They never wanted to admit or acknowledge this was happening to any of their church members past or present. Still, they were stuck believing that you sweep things like this under the rug and act like everything is okay when it wasn't.

Today, this young lady is a college graduate and a nurse. She is married with a son, living her best life. It was well worth me coming forward with my story of depression and thoughts about suicide because the good Lord allowed me to help someone.

My mother wanted to have a stroke. Me admitting that I had contemplated suicide truly upset her. She always thought I had it all together, but I never wanted to place my burdens on my parents. They were always helping others, and I didn't want to add to that. So, I kept things to myself. I placed a smile on my face and put one foot in front of the other, praying my way forward, showing them exactly what I wanted them to see. My mother apologized, feeling like she failed. Of course, none of this was her fault. She helped me develop into the woman I am today. She is an amazing mother who loves me unconditionally. The fact that she was willing to understand my condition and be there for me when I fell meant everything to me. She is why I strive to be the best mother possible to my own children.

Mental illness has been challenging in more ways than one. I feared passing it down to my own children, and I prayed that wouldn't happen. As much as we would like to shield our children from something like this, we can't. Mental illness can be inherited. Unfortunately, my children are affected by this as well.

All my children have had thoughts of suicide. Their reasons for that are so broad. And that's the thing about mental illness, one thing can push you over the edge and make you consider attempting suicide.

Looking back at the goodness of the Lord still brings me to tears because things could have gone another way. If you would have told me this would be my outcome, I wouldn't have believed you. Was it easy? Absolutely not. But I want to use my experience to be a catalyst for something that's swept under the rug, especially in the African American community. I know I'm stronger. I never knew I had such strength, but God gives you peace and power during times you don't think you can get through. Trust me, I can't believe how some of the most tragic events in life has propelled me forward to an understanding I wouldn't have been able to reach if I went down another road. Only God is all I can tell you. The lyrics from Greg O'Quin 'N Joyful Noize's song, *I Told the Storm* says,

"No weapons formed against me shall prosper. I don't have to worry about a thing. I'm more than a conqueror through Jesus Christ and he's gon', bring me out alright, yes, He is. It's amazing grace that's brought me safe thus far and grace is gonna lead me home. I stood on solid ground and told my storm and you need to tell your storm today..."

This song is my story and that of many individuals dealing with mental illness and thoughts of suicide, and it has kept me moving forward. My illness has been my storm, one I will battle with for the rest of my life. But with God, I know he will carry me through.

About the Author

Tresser Henderson was born and raised in a small Virginia town. She always wanted to write but put it off to further her education and went on to achieve an Associate Degree in Computer Medical Administration. A crossroad in her life changed her outlook on the future, and someone helped her realize writing was the God given talent she was supposed to pursue. Not letting this opportunity slip away again, Tresser stepped out on faith and pursued her dreams, penning the fiction *My Man's Best Friend*.

New York Times bestselling author Carl Weber recognized her talent and signed her to his publishing company, Urban Books through Kensington Publishing. The author of the *My Man's Best Friend* series, *Big Girls Drama*, and *The Johnson Sisters*, *Null & Void* is Tresser's first Christian novel. She also published *A Brother's Divide* under her own publishing company, Personify Publishing.

Broadening her horizon, she joins a group of talented woman for this anthology, *She Overcame Suicide* (SOS), concentrating on an issue rarely discussed in the African American community.

Candid about her past struggles with depression and thoughts of suicide, Tresser has participated in multiple motivational speaking engagements on the topic to help others.

Tresser is proving there are no limits to what you can do. With faith and God in your

corner, it is never too late to make your dreams
come true.

CHAPTER 7

How Did I Get Here?

D. Marie

One moment, it felt like I woke up depressed, wanting life to end, but that wasn't the case at all. How did I get here? Something happened. Something changed my mindset about life. Something was broken. It wasn't just overnight that life no longer held any meaning to me. From the outside looking in, everything was perfect. I had a husband, a child, a house. I was in school for biblical studies and serving in ministry, but something was still broken. How did I get here?

Leading up to the day of my attempt, home life was strange. Money was funny, arguing was at an all-time high and the days of my husband coming home were few. I was extremely overwhelmed as a young mother and wife trying to understand what it took to be all that I was at twenty years old. I had lost my way. How did I get here?

February 25th, 2015, it seemed like my world officially crashed on that snowy Wednesday. It was another day my husband didn't come home. Another day that one of the utilities in our home was still off. Another day of trying to figure everything out on my own (at least that's how I felt). My son and I were staying with a friend, and to this day, I cannot recall where my ex-husband was staying. Things were going as well as it could for everything that was going on in my life at that time. That specific day, I was with my best friend, my son and her family. The snow kept us inside most of the day, but that evening, we decided to go to Walmart. I hadn't talked to my husband much that day and decided to give him a call. What I thought would be a simple "check-in" turned into him telling me that he no longer wanted me and that I wasn't enough for him. I was shattered. The only person that I ever NEEDED to love me – didn't. On top of everything else in my life that never made sense, his rejection took the cake.

The end of that phone call felt like the end of my life. I was tired of being mistreated by everyone, tired of not feeling valuable to anyone, tired of feeling overwhelmed, tired of being tired. I had prayed and prayed for a marriage that never seemed to get better and I felt forsaken by God. In my mind, I made the decision that death was easier than continuing to live. I used the last two percent of battery life on my phone to text: **Pray for me** to every preacher, pastor and person of spiritual influence in my phone. And, as soon as the message sent, my phone died. My best friend offered to give me a "happy pill" (Klonopin) to calm me down and let me sleep off what had just happened.

After many tears, and what felt like the longest car ride of my life, we arrived back at her home. We unloaded the groceries in the kitchen, and she went to the medicine cabinet to get my "happy pill". I never knew that I could minimize my whole life to a moment of pain, trauma, heartbreak, confusion, and abandonment, but in that moment, all I knew was I didn't want to live anymore and taking as many pills as I could was going to be my one-way ticket out of here. I took the bottle from her hand and poured as many pills as I could into my hand, but she told me no and made me put some back. I pretended to put them all back, but when she wasn't looking, I slid them into my pocket. I gave her the bottle back and took the one pill as she suggested, washing it down with my Monster energy drink.

I sat my son on a blanket in the middle of the living room floor and gave him a kiss before turning towards the door. I said, "Take care of my son while I'm gone," and walked out. Though I had no real destination, my friend's neighborhood was familiar to me. I just knew that by the end of the night someone was going to find me in the snow. I walked closer into the neighborhood I was raised in, continuing to pop the pills that were in my pocket along the way. My phone was still dead, so I decided to walk to the neighborhood park to plug my phone up and lie down on the bench. I arrived at the park and tried to plug my phone in, but for some reason the outlets weren't working there. I was about six pills in when they started to catch up with me, and I decided to go to my other best friend's house to plug my phone up for the remaining time I had before the pills completely took me out.

Thankfully, she was up and thank God she answered. I plugged up my phone so it could charge. I knew I was displaying signs of being drunk or possibly high. Eventually, everything became cloudy, but this is how I remember that night. I was a mess, and when I turned my phone back on, there were lots of texts and calls. My friends would call, and my speech would be slurred. Then, my mother would call, and I would act perfectly fine because I didn't want her to worry about me, while still slipping a pill here and there until my best friend came and took them from me. Somehow, three great friends of mine found out where I was and came to me.

I remember someone being called and something being said about how I needed to get to the hospital immediately with the number of pills I had ingested. I crumbled into the snow, terrified that the world would know what I had done. I worried people would see me as an unfit and unstable mother, and they would think less of me as a Christian. I thought people would call me crazy. All these things plagued my already cloudy mind, and it felt like every single pill hit my system at once. From the back seat of the car, on the way to the hospital, I heard people praying to the same God I had earlier given up on. My eyes began to roll in the back of my head, and I was in and out of consciousness. I remember seeing a bright light, like you hear about in the movies, and at that moment I knew I was done. My life was over, I got what I thought I wanted.

When I came to myself, I was in the hospital and extremely angry because I had failed. I was mad at the doctors and nurses, at my friends for saving me, at anyone who thought my "terrible" life was worth living. Thankfully, they didn't have to pump my stomach, but they were going to send me to a psych ward for a few days until I could prove to be okay and get off of suicide watch. I wasn't having that. What did I look like going to a psych ward?

My husband came to the hospital and expressed how dumb and careless my actions were, then got up to leave. But I didn't want him to leave. I wanted him to turn around and tell me I was going to be okay. That we were going to be okay. But that didn't happen, he kept walking. And I, still inebriated, got out of the hospital bed to chase after him and tell him goodbye. Unfortunately for me, the hospital thought I was trying to run away, and the doctors called security to detain me and filed a

T.D.O   (Temporary   Detention   Order/
Involuntary Hospitalization).

Again, I was distraught, hurt and medicated. I started throwing chairs, trying to fight the officers in an attempt to free myself. All I wanted to do was tell my husband bye. The look on my family's face was devastating. They were scared for me and they were hurting. The hurt I was feeling spilled over to them. The next morning, they handcuffed and shackled me and had an officer take me to the psych ward. There, I realized there were people who were truly worse off than I was. Some people there were fighting harder than I was, but for some reason, God saw fit to make us all survivors. Even when we tried to rip the gift of life from ourselves, he still chose us. After three days of complying, taking meds and getting visits from worried family members and friends, I was released. I didn't leave happy and I didn't leave delivered – but I was alive.

I knew God worked in mysterious ways because I later found out that if I hadn't been drinking the Monster energy drink while taking the pills, I would have overdosed much sooner. Possibly when I was alone and when my phone was dead. The klonopins were slowing my heart rate down, but the energy drink was keeping it up. GOD IS GOOD!

Here I am today, four years past that moment and writing this has given me the time reflect and ask myself once again, "Desiree, how did you get there?" In the midst of situations, we hardly take time to reflect on what really led up to that specific moment – we just deal where we are. For a long time, I was stuck in the repetitive cycle of "yearly depression," and every year, I would get hit with the same emotions - stronger than the time before. Each time, I would convince myself that my life was not worth living and make an attempt...AGAIN. As you can tell, every attempt was unsuccessful, but I never gave God full reign over my life. I was in church, dancing and speaking in tongues, but never really turning the issues I faced fully over to God. Embarrassed for anyone to see me broken because I was SUPPOSED to be happy, I did everything I could to save face. I was supposed to have it all. All the while, from my childhood to marriage, life had left me empty. I was broken, and I was honestly terrified to see what it took to be repaired. When I asked God to help me deal and help me unpack those places I had hidden in my life, I was healed. I finally came to a place where I understood my life had value, and God loved me enough to love me when I didn't love myself and to CHOOSE life when I chose death.

Today, I still reside in Roanoke, Virginia. My son is four-years-old and I am twenty-four years old. I am currently working towards becoming a certified life coach, and I no longer battle suicidal thoughts or take antidepressants. Daily, I remind myself of who I am and who God has created me to be. I'm better, I'm whole and I'm HEALED. I have grown in ministry, and I am preaching the gospel and telling the world that regardless of what circumstance says, life is still worth living.

I invite you to take a moment to reflect. Reflect on where you have been and where you currently are. Ask yourself, "How did I get here?" Ask God to help you deal with those hidden and masked places. Ask him to break the cycles. Ask him to make you whole. Walk fearlessly in your newness, no longer bound by the chains of depression and suicidal thoughts. You deserve freedom, and it belongs to you. Never fear, you will obtain it. GO AFTER IT!

About the Author

Desiree Marie is an up and coming author. *She Overcame Suicide* is her first publication. She resides in Roanoke, VA, and is the mother of one son. A licensed evangelist, Desiree also has a movement called *Young but Chosen*. This movement is geared toward encouraging millennials to walk in their destiny and embrace their God-given calling. Desiree Marie also serves as a mentor and is currently working toward becoming a certified life coach.

CHAPTER 8

Dear Mr. Police Officer

Genisha Morton

"Mr. Police, please don't put the driver in jail. I ran into the street on purpose. It's not their fault. I wanted to die. Thank you!"

This was the letter I wanted to write when I was four, but what it actually looked like was probably scribble scrabble. At four years old, I was so angry inside. I didn't want to live anymore, and I couldn't take the pain from the beatings nor could I handle the fact that I had sex. I had no idea what it was, it just hurt like hell. I screamed as high and as loud as I could, and I haven't been able to scream since. I think something broke in my throat. I decided I wasn't going to live anymore and came up with a plan.

Now that I think about it, if I had known better, it would have worked. God covered me in my ignorance, and it failed. I packed my clothes and my brother's clothes because we were going to my aunt's house. I was going to leave my brother at my aunt's house and leave out of her apartment building and run into traffic. I was scared, but I felt like it couldn't be worse than the pain I was experiencing at home. But all my plans were canceled when my mom walked in on me packing and made me unpack our clothes. I was so furious that I didn't leave sooner. I felt like I took too long packing. *What did I pack my clothes for?* I didn't need any clothes where I was going. I was dreading my fifth birthday, and I barely sang the happy birthday song. I was sure my dad could tell I really didn't want to be there.

Since then, it became my personal goal to commit suicide successfully. I never felt wanted, loved, or accepted. I never felt like I belonged, and life didn't get better as I got older. The abuse was worse, I've been raped more times than I cared to count, and I've been bullied at school, home, and church. It seemed everywhere I went, people focused more on what was wrong with me than what was good about me.

I attended Cary Reynolds Elementary School, and the first thing I heard when I said hello was, "You're black." I promise I thought they were joking, but they were not. I told them about my grandfather's funeral, and they said I was a liar. The teacher even called my mother and said that I said things I hadn't said. I probably should've kept quiet, even the teachers joined in on teasing me. I was beat up daily by a redhead boy who I believe was abused himself. No one would stop him except one teacher when I was in the fifth grade. Actually, my fifth-grade year, he said he liked me a little just not to look at him. I told him every day that Jesus loved him, and he didn't have to be mean. He didn't believe me at first, but I believe he started to believe me in fifth grade because he left me alone and started picking on someone else. When he started picking on a white girl with red hair, the school wanted to get involved and stop him.

We left there, and I thought, *finally I can go to a school and make friends*, but it didn't work out at my next school either. At that school, I was called medusa, child with the wild hair, retard, etc. When I went to church, I was called the leader of the ugly group, amongst other things. When I was home, I was called crossed toes (my big toe is over my middle toe slightly), ugly, retarded, the works.

When my cousin moved in with us, he began bullying me, threatening me with knives and threatening to kill my family in their sleep. He didn't rape me right away, but he made me have sex with other guys he'd bring to the house. If I didn't do what he said, he'd lie to my parents about something. And they believed him every time, so telling on him was out of the question. He would lie his way out of it. I don't know how old I was when he raped me the first time, but I do know between him and these other guys he brought in, I was having a lot of unwanted sex. He even pimped me out to a cousin at a family reunion one year. I was relieved when he had to move out. My dad caught him and another guy raping me, but he blamed me for it. I would try to tell people, especially at church, but no one listened. Eventually, I realized they were telling my mother and she would say I was lying.

I was in the seventh grade and tired of trying. I didn't understand why this was happening to me, and I'd gotten saved before we moved to Georgia. I believe my dad got caught because he hurt someone who told. I was confused and felt like if no one loved me or wanted me around, then I was out. I wrote a letter, and somehow my mom found it, or the school told her, but she laughed at it. I was determined to make a believer out of them, so when I was home alone, I turned on the oven and put my head inside. As a kid who didn't really know what they were doing, somehow the pilot didn't light and the gas didn't turn on.

My sister came in the house with the biggest smile. She called me Doyesha because she couldn't say my name yet. It made me so happy, I decided I would wait. I was really hoping there wouldn't be a reason for me to try again, but things got worse. I would sing and pray all the time. I studied my bible constantly trying to be everything God said I should be, hoping that if I was good, the pain would stop, but I was never good enough, and no one liked me or wanted me around. The only value I added to anyone's life was to do what I was told and give them stuff. As long as I did that and never stood up for myself, I was considered a blessing and a good girl. At some point, between the ages of eleven and thirteen, I miscarried, and to this day, I still miss who I believe was my little girl. I don't know if it was my dad's or my cousin's or any of the other guys I had to have sex with.

I was done with life, I felt like I wasn't going to amount to anything, so I contemplated suicide again. This time, I read a book about a girl who seemed to feel like I did. At the end of it, she cried, "I just want someone to love me." In her story, cutting had been her way through pain, so I tried it myself. It worked! No more emotional pain. One time, I cut the word loser into my arm, and I thought I was going to die. I never knew I could bleed so much, but it healed, and nothing happened. I decided the easiest way would be to go to sleep and refuse to wake up. I felt like I was pushed awake the next day. I was pushed so hard, I felt the springs in the bed. I jumped up and asked who pushed me, but no one answered. I got up and ran into my mother's room screaming, "Who pushed me?" My sister denied it, and I'm not sure, but maybe she was telling the truth.

Things never got better, and I didn't do that well in school. The bullying seemed to follow me no matter where I went, and it was out of this world. I figured something was wrong with me, and everyone saw it but me. I was always depressed and didn't realize that I had become so negative I was impossible to be around. I graduated high school and attended Georgia State University hoping that I could be great. I wanted to put my past and the bullies and all of the abuse behind me. I wanted to escape and get away, but when I turned nineteen, I was raped again. The same day of my rape, I went to a job interview and was sexually harassed by the head manager, the one you were supposed to report inappropriate activity to. I was so uncomfortable, I quit. Everyone blamed me and said I should have dealt with the harassment and not quit my job, but I didn't understand why I had to deal with it. I was also told it would happen again, so I've been looking over my shoulder every day hoping that today is not the day.

When my sons were babies, I pressed charges against my dad for the sexual abuse, but I lost and we ended up homeless. I couldn't deal with fighting alone, so I lied and said I didn't remember something that I did. I followed my best friend to Kentucky, but nothing was going the way I needed it to, and I figured the boys would be better off with real parents. I'd already had arrangements with a set of parents so they wouldn't grow up like me. I swallowed a whole bottle of painkillers, but they did nothing. It was as if God deactivated them, even the doctors said they weren't strong enough.

On August 3, 2017, we were losing our house due to no fault of my own. I was tired of losing and not being productive the way I fought to be. I was doing everything I was supposed to do, and it wasn't good enough. I tried to cut my wrist but couldn't get a real grip on the knife. I was so frustrated, I threw the knife across the room, and suddenly had a flash of a friend "letting her hair down" and smiling. I figured if she could fight her depression and come out smiling, so could I.

I've been determined since then to let go of suicide as the answer. I decided I was going to fight back with my whole heart. I was in church singing, drama club, teaching, etc., and the church made me feel like talking about the things that hurt me was wrong. I felt that if I said anything (which I did often), I would be chastised for bringing everyone down. No one seemed to care about what I was going through, which made me feel like no one wanted me around. Feeling like no one loved me was the biggest issue that fueled my desire to commit suicide. Now, I love me and I want to survive so that I can be all that God has called me to be. He loves me, and that's all that matters.

About the Author

Creatively writing her way through life, Genisha Morton is known for being a woman of many talents. Singing and writing are tools she's used to cope with the events of her life. Most recently, she has completed two-thirds of a three-part series entitled, *My Life in a Dream!* Each story takes its turn telling the tale of a dream she had concerning her life. On December 1, 2018, she successfully held a book signing/launch party at the AWAKE coffee shop where she autographed and sold fifteen copies.

In addition to writing, Genisha has also spent time in a music studio recording music for her first album slated for release in the summer of 2019.

Along with writing and singing, Genisha has become more health conscience and is opening an online restaurant. Her goal is to have a fun place to interact with healthy food and family. She wants to be able to give to those who need it most and realizes that a millionaire has more than one source of income. Genisha is on the move creating wealth, prosperity, and good health.

Her goal is to leave not only a legacy, but an inheritance for her children and future generations. She has successfully raised three (four, if you count her nephew) young gentlemen into successful college students. These young men will also take part in her growing businesses so they can carry on their family's generational legacy long after she is gone. Her sons are her greatest joy and success, and they are constantly achieving goals that make her a very proud mom.

CHAPTER 9

I Survived!

Walikqua Johnson

There were many times when I wanted to end it all. At one point, I really thought I had nothing to live for. I hadn't accomplished much and was in a dark place with life. I was still going to church, singing on the praise team and in the choir and was beginning to preach. You would say this should have been a great time with all I was involved in concerning church, but outside of church, I was miserable. I was in a place of pretending to be happy, and on the inside, I was hurting. Around this time, I was in my teenage years. Many young people go through so much and adults don't know it or aren't aware or simply don't even care.

I remember a time when I was going through some difficult times with my mother and I was outside thinking, *why? Why me? Why did we have to argue and fight so much?* I wasn't a bad child but for some reason we always got into it. One particular time, I took some pills that I was taking to gain weight and to sleep. I intentionally took more than I was supposed to. I figured if I took the pills, I would fall asleep and just die. I laid down on the living room couch after taking the pills, and a few minutes later, I stood and stumbled towards the door, very dizzy. My vision was blurred, and my words were slurred. My nephew's father, who was staying with us at the time, asked if I was okay and my response was not clear at all. My lips wouldn't allow me to get my words out clearly. I remember walking out the door, but I can't remember what happened from there. All I know is that when I came to my mother was calling my name and shaking me so I could snap out of it. Eventually, the fog from the pills wore off, but as I reflect back on what could have really happened, I could have ended my life. I could have died right there in my mother's home. I never thought about how she would have felt finding her daughter dead. I was being selfish, but I was miserable because my father had passed away and I never got a chance to grieve.

I wasn't doing very well in school, academically or socially. I hung out with the wrong crew and was always getting into fights that landed me in the principal's office even though it wasn't my fault. Since I couldn't pass the New York City regents exams, I ended up dropping out and started dating these no good "church dudes." I got a job working fast food at McDonalds and White Castle and quit them both because it wasn't for me. I was always getting put out of my mother's house for something, so I was in and out of different homeless shelters or living from one person's house to the next. All of this stuff was happening, and I felt like I couldn't escape it. Don't get me wrong, I have some great childhood memories. Most of this stuff started after my dad died.

I recall another time I wanted to commit suicide but didn't actually go through with it. I just had the thoughts running through my mind. This is when I began to try to fix my situation. I didn't want to be that suicidal person in the family, the one known for trying to die. You know there's always that one person in the family who's "crazy", the black sheep. I didn't want that to be me, and I was too embarrassed to allow people to know what I was feeling or going through. As I reflect, I probably should have gotten professional help. It's amazing how we allow what others may think, or say about us, stop us from doing what we need to do. I just thank God for never leaving my side even when I wanted to leave him.

Be strong and of good courage, fear not, nor be afraid of them: for the LORD thy God, he it is that doth go with thee; he will not fail thee, nor forsake thee (Deuteronomy 31:6, KJV).

I thank God because during that time of depression, I found myself doing things I wouldn't normally do, like sleeping around. I thought it made me happy because it took my focus off my issues for a little while, but then I was back to being homeless and running from place to place. I really have to give God all the glory. If it wasn't for Him, I honestly don't know where I would be at this point in my life. He saved me for real. By his grace, I am saved and I'm happy about it. It is amazing how you can be a Christian and still have these kinds of thoughts. Surely we must practice what we preach. I can now say that overcoming suicide is a milestone and one thing I can talk to others about. Young women go through so much and most of the time have no one to talk or vent to. No one to give them godly advice and wisdom.

I'm glad I'm in a place where I can talk about this after being in denial so long. I'm no longer ashamed of having those thoughts or taking those pills to end my life. But I am glad I serve a mighty good God who thought enough of me to allow me to keep living and keep pushing. I'm married with two beautiful children. I went back to school, earned my bachelor's degree and have recently enrolled for my master's degree.

I almost gave all that up because I was too afraid to talk to someone. Too afraid to trust God and trust the process. Too afraid to activate my faith. ***Now faith is the substance of things hoped for, the evidence of things not seen (Hebrews 11:1, KJV).*** Too afraid to just believe in myself and believe that God had my back the entire time. So many times, I felt alone. I thought God had left me, but he was there all along. Many days, it was me who strayed. When I think about it, I never went without a meal. I never went without proper clothing on my back. I never went without bathing or brushing my teeth. I never went without a place to lay my head, and I truly thank God.

My goal now is to give back, give back to women young and mature. To be a listening ear. Be the person who can speak encouraging words and uplift their spirits. My goal is to promote change within ourselves by first transforming our minds. We don't have to end up where we started. We can do better if we desire better. You are not what people say you are. I want to inspire women all over to be confident in who they are. Be comfortable in their own skin. Secure a job and turn it into a thriving career— skills no one can take away from them. I want to help women become writers, entrepreneurs, and be passionate about what they are doing. I want us to know it is okay to cry. It is okay to feel weak and burnt out but whatever we do, NEVER give up. Keep pushing forward and know that God is right there every step of the way. Remain prayerful and understand the power behind praying and fasting.

About the Author

Lady Walikqua M. Johnson is a Bronx native who relocated to North Carolina in 2017. Prior to relocating, she was an NYPD Explorer and an active member of Higher Praise Community Church. During this time, she realized she was called to preach the gospel and was made a youth minister. Lady Walikqua later left that ministry and became an active member of Road To Damascus Ministry of God, Inc. where she sat and served under the leadership of Pastor Eugene Johnson and Co-Pastor Doris Johnson. There, she had her trial sermon and began to preach the gospel.

She has devoted her life to help see the people of God healed, restored and set free from bondage of past hurts and distresses. Her passion goes beyond the four walls of ministry. Her vision is to reach and help young and mature women grow spiritually. Lady Walikqua presides over the Leaning Towards a Better Me Council, which she founded.

She received her Bachelor's of Science Degree for Healthcare Administration from ECPI University in January 2019. She loves the medical field, and her passion is helping people no matter what.

Lady Walikqua serves alongside her husband Bishop Anthony P. Johnson I of Unity Cathedral Church & Greater Vision Church. Lady Walikqua Johnson is grateful for all that God has done in her life, though nothing compares to the joy of life with her devoted husband, Bishop Anthony Johnson and their three sons: Royal, Prince and Phillip, and their beautiful daughter, Dymond.

CHAPTER 10

Refined

Tamara Harris

I assumed everyone hated me, because I had all the pretty dresses and the best of the best. Everything was done for me before I could think about it. Even though I was only six years old, I pretended to be happy, even when I wasn't. As a teen, I managed to hold sadness in for so long, it almost killed me. I was angry, I didn't want this life, nor did I want to share my parents, and I didn't feel like God heard me. I didn't feel like I belonged here because I struggled to fit in, trust or even believe I could have just one friend. Every time I walked into the room, it was as if I could feel the whole church staring at me and I could hear the laughs. My palms would sweat instantly, and I would cringe. "God, if I could get out of here..." But, it was no use. I felt stuck, closed in and confused about who I was as an individual. I didn't want to be "the pastor's daughter", I just wanted to be me. I remember turning sixteen and finally realizing, I wasn't okay. I wasn't going to hold it in, and I couldn't fake another smile.

Finally, at age nineteen, I broke into a million pieces and I didn't even know why. I threw myself into alcohol, drugs, and sex, which led me to losing my faith, hope and trust in God. Everyone I thought I could depend on was not friends, and all I could do was tell God how much I was hurting. It got real with just me and him on this journey called life. Every day, I was mentally and emotionally drained from pretending. Every button had been pushed down to my soul, and I kept trying to rationalize everything that was going on in my life. My mind was completely disturbed by all the years growing up in church but missing God completely.

I knew ministry and the business aspect of church. I knew was what to be expected as a pastor's daughter, but I couldn't tell you about God. I had no peace of mind and no freedom to express what I heard in my head because I had blocked it out. I wasn't at peace with myself. I had lived a life pleasing other people, and now I couldn't depend on anyone. I decided to leave everything I had, I left my church, family and friends. I sat in my apartment one day as I prepared for college classes, and the mental breakdown finally occurred. I saw the dark clouds hover over me like a gloomy storm as years of anguish rolled onto my shoulders.

After a long time fighting the fakeness, the urge hit me hard. I felt my heartbeat increase and my lungs constrict as I tried to exhale. I couldn't breathe, but at that moment, I didn't want to breathe. I felt the heavy rush of water to my eyes as my throat tightened. I begged God for a sign. "Please help me, I just want to die." I laid my head on my pillow, fighting misery and the urge to panic. No matter how much I wanted to find myself, there was no way I could do this, or anyone I could tell. *Would anyone understand? Would people say I'm crazy?* Though, the small still voice of the Holy Spirit talked to me daily, I had no idea what or who it was. The tricks my mind played on me was like a game of chess with the devil that I played every day. I saw visions and dreams in my head of things no one would understand. I couldn't sleep because of the nightmares and terrors. I felt nothing but agony, and I tried to confront it alone. I thought companionship was what I needed so I decided to marry at age twenty-one to stop the pain.

My first marriage was like being with a stranger. I knew nothing about him, and he knew nothing about me. The day after our wedding, he cursed a guy out for just talking to me about a pair of shoes in Foot Locker. I thought maybe he was being protective like a husband should be. Then, the next week there was an eruption which resulted in him leaving the house with no notice. I had no idea where he went, but each time he wanted to walk out, I tried to fix it. Why did he leave? Did I misunderstand him? Did I say something? At twenty-one years old, I didn't know the first thing about communication. I came into marriage with no responsibilities and no experience, but I learned more in the first five months of marriage than I could handle. The more he walked out, the more rejection I felt. Finally after six months, I found out I was pregnant and he left, blaming me for his exit.

I sat on my bed looking at the pills. My heart was racing, and I couldn't breathe. Pain was all I had known my whole life. In agony, I laid across the bed and grabbed my chest as I sobbed constantly. I pressed my palms against my temple as thoughts from years and years of torment rushed through my head. *You are not going to survive this, so just do it. Do it and get it over with because no one will ever care that you are gone.*

In the background, I could hear my kids laughing and playing. Innocently, they laughed, not even knowing what I was doing in the next room. I felt out of control, disappointed and ruined by the constant arguments, accusations, and distrust in my marriage. I had wanted to be with this man so bad. Even after he left me during the pregnancy, when we reconnected, I felt alive again. He was my safety net from all the denial I felt. He told me things that made me feel like I was the best thing that ever happened to him. On the other hand, he also made me feel like I was the reason for all his problems. I could never understand why I couldn't do enough or say enough to make him love me like I needed him to. Maybe something was wrong with me. Could I not be loved? Was I just a woman who could not fit into this world of love? I always thought God had punished me. I felt like I was the reason people rejected, abandoned and hurt me. There were so many unanswered questions in my head.

No one ever made me feel like I could do anything. I had rushed into marriage twice before. I felt like taking the pills would make it all go away. Maybe someone else could be a better mother to my children than I could. I felt unworthy of my children because I was being so selfish. *Look at their little innocent faces looking at me without a care in the world. God, why would you give me these two precious gifts if I can't be mentally stable?* I hated myself even more as I sat there contemplating taking the pills. The mental struggle was suffocating me, and I was drowning in my own pain. I thought I would never amount to anything and that no one would even bother to care if I just ended it. I started to think about how I became who I currently was. Deep down, I wasn't okay. I was shattered, discouraged and I knew couldn't fix myself. Consumed in distrust, uncertainty and terror, the enemy had my mind. Fear kept me from being delivered, but God was still there.

For me, being unvalued was a drastic understatement, especially when thoughts in my head were not the way people perceived me. Most of the time, people thought I was arrogant, a snob. They'd say, "Oh, she thinks she is "cute."" When I looked in the mirror, I didn't see the girl everyone thought I was. I saw loneliness, pain, shame and anger. I was not even the girl I wanted to be. I was running from something that I couldn't escape. I had lost myself in quicksand and all I wanted to do was sink. Maybe if I sank, it would be better. Maybe sinking was the only way to escape. But what if I wanted to come up? I had no idea what would be better but if I could tell someone, I could try to explain.

I sat there looking at those pills, thinking, *I hate my life.* Half a bottle of Motrin 800 milligrams stared back at me as I contemplated what to do. I cried until I couldn't breathe. I took them, told God I was sorry and laid back across the bed. I was sorry for disappointing everyone, including my kids, but I knew this was the best way. I started to feel drowsy, and then I couldn't feel my hands or feet. I barely opened my eyes and the room was spinning above my head. *What was I thinking?* But, it was too late, I couldn't turn back.

I opened my eyes to my best friend shaking me. "Tammy! Tammy! Can you hear me? Get up! What did you do?" Barely able to comprehend or open my mouth, somehow, I managed to say, "Huh?"

She said I texted her from my phone, but I had no idea what she was talking about. I felt cold towels on my body, thankful my friend was a nurse and knew what to do. The last thing I heard my friend say was, "We need to get her to the hospital!"

I woke up, dazed and confused, in a hospital bed. I stared at the wall, not knowing where my kids were or what was going on. Little did I know, somehow a text message that said: **come**

get me was sent to my friend. I knew that was a sign from God. I was home alone with the kids, and no one could have sent that text message if I was out. I didn't know why, but I didn't ask questions anymore. God immediately said to me, "Tamara, you have purpose. It was not time yet." What I failed to realize was that I wasn't meant to be accepted. I was meant to be misinterpreted so God could keep me exactly where He needed me, understood by Him. When I came into this glorious revelation, I walked away from my second marriage, free, happy and ready to walk with God.

"She is getting married again?" Someone asked someone else, in reference to my third marriage. I was embarrassed, of course. But this time, I felt love for real. I had met this wonderful man, Marcus, who made me laugh, smile and live like a kid all over again. I just wanted to be happy and not judged. Marcus did that for me, he didn't judge me at all. He was the first person who looked at and saw purpose in me. Even though I was hurting inside, I still felt loved. God brought Marcus to show me love through Him. The day I almost died was the day God caught me, stood me up and gave me the ability to finally stand. I began to write, cry, write and release the anger from within. One day, I wrote so much, I looked and said, "Oh my goodness, this is my book!" I had written one hundred pages of my whole story and released all the years that I felt was for nothing. My first book, *The Refinement Process*, showed me how all the things I went through was to provoke me into purpose. Since then, I have never looked back because I've been refined.

About the Author

Tamara Marie Harris is the CEO of Empower University, pastor of Divine Empower Ministries and daughter of Deborah Ministries and has currently published five books. She is a wife, mother, and daughter of Dr. Dennis Winborn and Dr. Paula Hill. And by faith, she has become a best-selling and nominated author, entrepreneur, mentor, vision strategist and ordained minister. Tamara was born and raised in the church as a pastor's kid and began to write at a young age. At the age of twelve, she gained inspiration for her first play. By age seventeen, she was teaching bible study and Sunday school and mentoring others by age twenty-two.

Pastor Tamara follows the call of the Lord, hosting empowerment conferences and preaching and imparting purpose into others through the Holy Spirit. As she shares her testimony of overcoming depression, suicide, divorce, molestation and alcohol abuse, her ministry has grown into healing for many. Pastor Tamara continues to empower others by showing them how to walk in faith and turn their pain into purpose.

Tamara was nominated in the 2017 IALA awards for "author on the rise" and for best-selling author in the *Stories from the Pink Pulpit: Women in Ministry Speak* anthology. She has also been awarded a doctor of practical theology certificate, a licensed teaching credential by the state of Illinois, and a master certification in social media marketing, business management and leadership training.

CHAPTER 11

I Made It On Broken Pieces

Alma Thomas

How many of us have looked back over our lives and realized it was only by God's grace that we made it through every obstacle, disappointment, failure and storm? On this journey called life, we are faced with difficult situations and challenges. Often times, during these struggles, we don't see how it is humanly possible to make it out victoriously. The enemy will speak to us and make us feel like this is our final chapter. We try everything, but it appears like everything that we try fails.

Life has a way of throwing curveballs, and oftentimes we cry out, "Lord, why is it so much pain? Why me?" We question God about why we were diagnosed with cancer or why we can't pay our bills. One question I personally asked God was why did my son have to leave his earthly home for his heavenly home at the tender age of eighteen? I relied on my favorite passages of scriptures to help me to get through one of my greatest storms of my life.

Everyone faces some kind of storm in life. Some storms are natural disasters such as tornadoes, hurricanes or blizzards. Others are personal storms such as loss of a job, loss of a loved one, setbacks or relationship problems. Unfortunately, they are all a part of this journey called life. Therefore, we understand that in this life we are going to face many storms. The question is not whether or not we are going to go through storms in life, but the question is, as we cope with storms in life, how can we be unstoppable despite the storms of life?

In the passage of scripture (Acts 27:27-28), Paul is imprisoned and on his way to Rome to stand trial. Paul warns them that it is not safe to travel at this time of the year, but they ignore his warning and take the trip anyway. How many times have we decided we are grown and don't have to listen to anyone, refusing to listen to sound counsel? We have the mindset that we are going to do things our way. Like when we were children, and our parents told us not to touch the stove because it was hot, but we had to touch the stove and get burned to truly believe the stove was hot. Often times in life, God will tell us not to do something, and we go against the will of God finding ourselves in a storm. How much grief and pain would we have saved ourselves if we listened to the voice of God? The sailors did not listen to Paul. After all, who did he think he was, he was just a prisoner.

Many times in life, we go astray because we look at the package that is carrying the message. The men didn't listen to Paul, and consequently they sailed right into the worst storm of their life. They tried everything to save the ship. When nothing worked, they started throwing everything they didn't need overboard. Many of us are traveling through life with excess baggage. We picked this baggage up from every storm we ever went through in life. Although the ship was destroyed, the men all survived, albeit some on broken pieces.

In 2009, I went through one of the fiercest storms of my life. I lost my son. The devil told me I might as well throw in the towel because this storm was going to take me out. He told me that I had preached my last sermon. He also asked me how I could mentor young people when my own child was gone. My son had been the choir director, so I couldn't stand to hear the choir sing anymore. I couldn't bear to speak to any of my friends who still had their children. I was on the verge of cussing out the next person who told me my son was in a better place. I did not want to hear one more person say he was in a better place. I was tired of it! At the end of my rope, on April 17, 2009, I was going to end it all and meet my son in "that better place." I stood alone in my sister's kitchen holding two bottles of high blood pressure pills. As I poured the contents of the bottles into my hand, I was crying hysterically and asking God why he didn't just take me instead of my son. I heard a small whisper, "If you do this, you will never see him again. You are not ready to go."

On that day, I put those pills down and slowly began my long road to recovery. It was not easy, because I made a lot of permanent decisions while I was in a temporary place. I was broken but not destroyed. I was wounded but I made it. You can still see the scars, but I made it. Many nights in the midnight hour, I have cried all night long asking God why I endured so much pain. I have not always been perfect but I have been faithful. There were things I endured in my life — physical, mental and verbal abuse as a child, the loss of my child, and a failed marriage. Many people would have never made it through these storms. The storms would have killed them. They should have killed me but thank God, I made it! According to man, I should not still be here, I should have never made it through the harsh storms of life, but God had a plan for my life. My destiny was waiting for me.

I remember telling God I wanted to be anointed, not really knowing the anointing was going to cost me something. God asked me how bad I wanted it. Did I want it bad enough to weather the storms that were going to come? I made it through the storms unstoppable but on broken pieces.

The one lesson I learned as I was in the midst of my storms is that not everyone wants you to make it out of your storm. Through much pain, I discovered you cannot share your dreams with everyone. There are going to be times in your life when you have to plant your dreams in secret and water them with your tears in the midnight hour. There are people who have been placed in your life to be dream killers, and they do not want you to survive your storm. They are waiting and watching for you to drown in your storms.

After the death of my son, my friends, and even my family, thought I was not going to make it through this storm. I did not want to preach from a place of hurt and anguish, so I took a sabbatical from preaching. I remember attending a women's conference during that time and the prophet prophesied to me, telling me God said I was going to make it. Not only was I going to make it out of this storm, but I was not going to look like what I had been through. The fire was not meant to consume me but to refine me. The prophecy continued with the Lord saying I was coming out of this storm blessed, coming out healed, coming out with more than I had at the beginning of the storm.

I realized I am unstoppable! The devil tried to stop me, but he realized he had to bring out his best artillery in order to stop my destiny. I learned that the greater the anointing, the harsher the storm. The storm set me free from conformability. The storm set me free from people and wondering what they thought about me. There were some things that were holding me back and it took the storm to set me free. The truth is there was some stuff I didn't want to get rid of, and it took the storm to get it out of me in order for me to truly be unstoppable. While I was in the storm, I realized that if I was going to go where I have never been before, I would have to do what I had never done before.

I thank you, devil, because you propelled me into my destiny and while I was in my storm, I perfected my praise and my dance. God will use our storms as a vehicle to benefit others around us. Our trials and tribulations help to develop and confirm our testimonies. How can I tell you can make it through a storm if I've never went through a storm and made it myself?

Somebody reading this book is going through a storm and your ship has been destroyed. In spite of this, don't give up. You are unstoppable! You will make it through the storm. I can see something floating in the water. It's a board. Further down, I can see a broken piece of a ship. Don't give up! Grab hold of it and float to land. You have been through a storm, but you made it. It should have killed you. It should have killed me, but praise God we are unstoppable! We made it on broken pieces, but we made it. Now it's time to step into our destiny. We are unstoppable!

About the Author

Alma Collins Thomas, a minister, author, motivational speaker, consultant and coach, is a mother of two: Tysean, who died in 2009, and Sabria. Alma is the founder and executive director of Alma Collins Thomas Ministries. For twenty-seven years, Minister Thomas worked at Amityville Head Start as a preschool teacher. Minister Thomas is a Suffolk County Girl Scout leader and volunteer at UNAYO Youth Center and Kingz Kidz Outreach Ministries. Minister Thomas attends the Church of Jesus Christ Our Lord where she presently serves as the youth director and special events planner.

Her two passions are working with youth and empowering women. Her favorite topic is purpose and helping people to find out why they are on this earth and living the life that God meant for us to live. Her favorite scripture is Jeremiah 29:11, and her favorite quote is "I don't feel no ways tired. I have come too far from where I started from. Despite all of the obstacles I have had to face in my life, I am still standing and I don't look like the hell I have been through."

CHAPTER 12

I Remember Dee

Desiree Johnson

Her name was Dee.

And I vividly remember the day I appeared in her life.

I was dressed to impress. My tattered, black cloak wrapped my body, hood covering my pale gray face (and my grin, of course).

Underneath it, I concealed every trick, mind game, and weapon I intended to give her.

My name is Suicide, and I always claim my victim.

When I approached her, her face turned cold and she completely stalled.

"Who are you?" She asked, with a slight tremble in her voice.

I could tell she was broken and sad. That was my moment. I hid my grin and whispered.

"I am just a friend, sweet girl. I can help you. Don't you want to know how?"

She was hesitant at first. I could tell, but no worries. I reached beneath my cloak and pulled out a bottle of pills.

"I know how you wish to be happy and escape this place. If you take one of these, that wish will surely come true. If you take all of them, then you can leave this place forever and never have to worry again."

She reached for those pills and I almost leaped with excitement! Then she began to cry. Puzzled, I asked her, "What's wrong, dear? Don't you want the pills?"

To which she replied,

"I know what will really happen to me if I take these pills. They will end my life. Even though I want to take them, I have to believe things will get better." She turned and walked away.

I was frustrated but not discouraged.

That trick might have failed but when I came back the next day, I had a WHOLE NEW game plan.

I could see that she was still sad...and ANGRY. I remember thinking, I can use that. I approached her again.

"I thought we could play a game today to help you release some of that anger."

This time she was slightly intrigued. "A game?" she asked. "What kind of game?"

I asked her to hold out her arm while I reached beneath my cloak and pulled out a blade.

"Use this blade. With each cut you make, some of your anger will pour out and you will feel better. If you're good, you'll win the prize of all your anger spilling out and never having to feel it again."

I knew I had her when she took the blade and pressed it to her arm. Right as she started to make the first cut, she paused, and I heard her whisper to herself what sounded like a proverb.

"Don't let how angry you are make you sin." she quoted, "Don't let your anger control you, not even for a day (Ephesians 4:26)."

"What does that mean? Aren't you tired of holding on to this anger?!" I pushed.

She handed me back the blade. "It means I can't do this. There are other ways for me to deal with my anger."

And then she turned and walked away for the second time.

I HAD NEVER had my tricks continuously fail. Usually by that point, I'd be hand in hand with my chosen, giving them the usual speech about how it was 'too late' and how what was 'done is done'.

Dee was smart, but I wasn't about to give up.

On the last day I approached her, I knew I would have her.

She was on her knees praying and crying. I could hear her shouting, "WHY ME!?" and "ARE YOU EVEN LISTENING?!" as if she were stuck on a loop. I knew I had to bring out the big guns.

I seized my moment.

"There, there, sweetie," I comforted. "I hear you and I have the same question. Is 'whomever' even listening? It's time to just end all of this. No more wondering if anyone is listening to your cries."

I reached beneath my cloak and pulled out a gun and placed it in her hand. My last trick. For a few moments, we both sat there in complete silence while she stared at the gun. I could see the desire to take my advice burning in her eyes. I could tell she was contemplating putting the gun to her chest and pulling the trigger...at least that's what I thought until she began to speak again.

"I know you don't have any power," she said to me. "For three days you've had this gun and could have just finished the job yourself. Yet you placed it my hand because you want ME to destroy MYSELF."

She stood from her praying position, still staring at the gun, right before pointing it towards me.

"Well, now, it's you who has been tricked. Do you know what I was praying for before you appeared today? I asked God why you keep trying to destroy me, and I asked him to give me strength to defeat you. When I asked him if he was even listening, he explained that I've always been stronger than you, and then you appeared again."

She lowered the gun and placed it back in my hand. I stood there in disbelief as she continued.

"This time, I am not afraid, and I know that you can only stay if I allow you to, and I refuse to give you power or anymore of my time. I refuse to take my own life knowing you want nothing more than for me to leave my family behind for your own gain. It's time for you to leave now."

So, there you have it.

They call her a survivor now because she escorted me out of her life and never looked back, but I never forgot about her.

She saw past all my trickery... pointed a gun at ME, SUICIDE, and demanded that I leave her alone!

What can I say?

She beat me at my own game. I can't forget Dee.

I'll never forget Dee.

About the Author

Desiree Johnson is a mother and a writer, born and raised in the Roanoke, Virginia valley. She is widely known for her infectious energy, creativity, and ability to easily make anyone smile or laugh.

At the very young age of nine years old, Desiree picked out her first journal and quickly discovered her knack for creating various types of stories and poetry. At that time, she had no idea that seeing someone's face glow by what she wrote would fuel her to keep writing for the rest of her life. Desiree graduated from Patrick Henry High School with honors in 2013, after giving birth to her son, Jaiden. Shortly after, she set off on her own for the first time to find her career calling and passion.

Since the age of nineteen, she has been proudly making her mark on the world as a successful banker and banker coach with Wells Fargo financial institution. Although she is most passionate about her career and being a full-time mother, she occasionally enjoys drawing, singing, and will never miss an opportunity to encourage or share her way of worship with others through praise dance.

Out of all her accomplishments, Desiree is most proud to say that she is a survivor. She's survived abusiveness, homelessness, and even struggled with mental instability but has never given up. Currently, she is partnering with others on projects to facilitate suicide prevention and mental health awareness.

Resources

Suicide Prevention Lifeline
Call 1-800-273-8255 or visit
http://suicidepreventionlifeline.org/

National Alliance on Mental Illness
(NAMI)
Call 1-800-950-6264 or email: info@nami.org

**Substance Abuse & Mental Health
Services Administration** (SAMHSA)
Call 1-800-662-HELP (4357)

Healthy Place
www.healthyplace.com

Made in the
USA
Columbia, SC